Original title:
Island Escape

Copyright © 2025 Creative Arts Management OÜ
All rights reserved.

Author: Arabella Whitmore
ISBN HARDBACK: 978-1-80581-576-1
ISBN PAPERBACK: 978-1-80581-103-9
ISBN EBOOK: 978-1-80581-576-1

Mirage of the Faraway

A coconut falls with a comical thud,
The local crabs dance in the sand-laden mud.
Seagulls squawk loudly, they're trying to chat,
While tourists sit still, all splashed in sun's hat.

The drinks are all shaking, the straws have a fight,
A blender's on strike, oh what a delight!
A sunburnt dad starts a limbo contest,
With a hippo-shaped float, oh we're so impressed!

Retreat into Blue

Flip-flops are flying, a splash and a cheer,
A dog chases seagulls with gusto and fear.
The snorkelers giggle, they can't find their fins,
While kids build sandcastles, adorned with dogkin.

A shady cabana holds whispered delight,
Where laughter erupts and the day feels just right.
The sun-flavored snacks dribble down a kid's chin,
In a race for the last slice, who'll finally win?

Serene Horizons

The hammock sways gently, a feline's quick nap,
A parrot chimes in with a gossip-filled clap.
Palm trees are swaying, they dance out of tune,
While a sun-worshiper dreams of winning a rune.

A crab in a cap tips his hat and bows low,
To a kid with a bucket, putting on a show.
Tanned legs in the air, yoga done wrong,
In a world where the laughter's the only true song.

The Untouched Shoreline

A clam with a mustache winks and confides,
That fish gossip daily, but human fish hides.
Footprints in sand tell of play and of fun,
While shadows are dancing, escaping the sun.

A race of weird sea-glass keeps the laughter alive,
While walruses giggle, this place is a thrive.
A sandy magician, a wizard of sun,
Turns lost flip-flops into treasures for fun!

Enchanted Waters

In waters blue like jellybeans,
I paddle on a flamingo's dream.
The fish wear hats, the ducks can dance,
Throwing my worries a second glance.

The sun is a disco ball, it seems,
As sea turtles join in wacky schemes.
With cocktails made of rainbow swirls,
I laugh as the ocean gently twirls.

Surfing on Tranquility

I ride the waves on a rubber duck,
Wobbling wildly, wishing for luck.
With every splash, I find my groove,
While seagulls scream, 'Get in the move!'

My surfboard's made of candy canes,
As jellyfish sing their sweet refrains.
The tide's a giggle, the breeze is bright,
Dancing on foam from morning to night.

A Quiet Revolt Against Reality

With coconuts, I start a coup,
Against the clock, we'll break right through.
In flip-flops, we march, a silly crew,
Planning to snack on the ocean's dew.

The hammock swings with laughter's cheer,
As sunburned noses draw us near.
Reality can take a break,
We'll toast to dreams with coconut cake!

Among Whispering Palms

Beneath the palms, where shadows play,
The squirrels are plotting—what a fray!
I've joined their ranks in this grand scheme,
To steal the sun and ride the beam.

The breeze whispers, 'Join in the fun!'
While parrots are shouting, 'Let's go run!'
With laughter echoing through the leaves,
We dance with joy, as dreams believe.

Uncharted Waters

Setting sail on soda pop,
Where jellyfish do the cha-cha,
The compass points to candy shop,
I think I've lost my llama.

The fish wear shoes and dance in pairs,
While crabs argue over french fries,
The sun's a pie in fun-filled flares,
And every wave a silly surprise.

Seagulls cackle with glee and flair,
Diving deep for chocolate cake,
I shout and laugh, wind in my hair,
Wishing for that silly mistake.

We trade our maps for frozen treats,
As dolphins join our merry crew,
In this crazy place, life's full of beats,
Just me, the sea, and a zebra, too.

The Allure of Distance

I packed my dreams in bubble wrap,
Boarded a boat made of cheese,
With every wave, I take a nap,
And wake to tea with bumblebees.

The horizon sings a zany song,
As octopuses juggle high,
While somewhere in the crowd, a prong,
Writes poems to the seagulls' sigh.

A treasure chest of silly hats,
What wonders in the deep await?
Cockatoos host their pirate chats,
We dance until the sun is late.

Oh, how the tides love to play tricks,
I find a map to nowhere fast,
And every twist just makes me mix,
In a whirlpool, I'm a merry blast!

Floating on Daydreams

On a raft made of marshmallow fluff,
I skim the surface with a grin,
Here clouds taste like popcorn - how tough,
To choose between sweet or sin.

An octopus plays a bongo drum,
While turtles wear the brightest shades,
The rhythm's wacky, the beat is dumb,
And all my worries gently fade.

With a sloth as my canoe guide,
We paddle slow, just taking time,
Finding joy in the silliest tide,
Every ripple, a quirky rhyme.

So let's float away on whimsy's trail,
With seagulls strumming a ukulele,
In this world where laughter sets sail,
And life's a playful, quirky ballet.

Dreams of Distant Horizons

A boat made of cardboard drifts with flair,
A captain in flip-flops, without a care.
With snacks piled high and drinks that are cold,
We sail to a place where adventures unfold.

The seagulls are laughing, they're part of the crew,
They dive for the chips, like they really knew!
With laughter and sand stuck deep in our toes,
We've traded our worries for ice cream cones.

Echoes of Stillness

The palm trees are whispering jokes to each other,
While crabs start a conga, oh what a bother!
Their dance is so silly, it tickles the sand,
As we join the fun, all awkwardly planned.

The sun's blazing bright, and my hat flies away,
Chasing it down like a game we must play.
With laughter and antics all under the sun,
We're a comedy troupe just trying to have fun.

Secrets on the Wind

The breeze carries secrets from far and wide,
Like tales of a mermaid with a pet that can glide.
Her fishy companion swims with a hat,
And he tells us stories that we laugh at!

A coconut falls with a thud and a splash,
"Hey, watch your head!" is the next funny crash.
With giggles around and sunburns that sting,
We tuck in for stories that laughter will bring.

Glistening Shores of Freedom

The waves are a party, the sand's full of glee,
As jellyfish waltz in the sun's jubilee.
We grab tiny shovels, build castles so tall,
A moat full of laughter surrounds them all.

A crab takes our flag, he's off with a cheer,
Our sandy domain's his new cozy lair!
With tickles and splashes and sun hats amiss,
We toast to the fun, not a moment to miss.

The Last Lighthouse

In a lighthouse, Henry's stuck,
His only friend, an old duck.
They trade jokes and tales so bright,
Waiting for the fading light.

Seagulls laugh at his retreat,
He builds a raft with old receipts.
Off he goes, with a feathery cheer,
Sailing far, but can't steer clear.

Oh, that duck can't hold its quack,
As waves come in, they drift back.
Home's not far, with shores so near,
He'll just stay till next year, dear.

Journey to the Untouched Sands

Pack a hat, don't forget the sunscreen,
Bill brought chips, but forgot the cuisine.
His drink's a mix of fruity mess,
A cocktail of clumsiness, I guess.

Out on the beach, they make a scene,
Building castles, like a king and queen.
For every wave that crashes down,
A little laughter hides the frown.

The sunburnt crew jumps in the tide,
Billing each other for each ride.
With sandy toes, they shout and play,
What a silly, sun-soaked day!

Tides of Solitude

Bobby sets out with snacks galore,
His fishing rod drags on the shore.
No fish in sight, just chips and chat,
He's more successful with a chatty chat.

The tide rolls in, it's quite a scene,
Bobby's boat floats, but it looks mean.
He waves to a crab, who scuttles away,
"Guess I'm all alone today!"

As dusk approaches, he makes a wish,
Would swap his rod for a tasty fish.
But silence reigns, waves gently clap,
Time for a snooze in his lopsided lap.

Shores of Respite

At the shore, Jane's clad in flair,
A wild mix of colors, quite the scare.
She trips on a towel, falls with flair,
Now she's a sandman without a care.

Tom's surfing, with no sense of grace,
Catching waves or just foam in space?
He wipes out hard, lands with a splat,
"Oh great, I'm now part of the mat!"

The sun sets low, too cool to leave,
They celebrate with laughs, which they weave.
On this beach, silliness will thrive,
In silly antics, they feel alive!

Alone in Seafoam

With a rubber duck, I float away,
Tangled in seaweed, having my play.
The seagulls squawk in a comedy show,
I wave back at fish, 'Are you in the know?'

Sunblock on my nose, I'm quite the sight,
Dancing with crabs in the shimmering light.
A jellyfish joins, with a wobbly dance,
Calling it 'jelly', while I take a chance.

Horizon's Embrace

A horizon so wide, I lost my shoe,
The tide tickles toes, 'What else is new?'
Hats flying high as a breeze takes a spin,
I chase after waves, laughing at my win.

But wait! What's that? A flip-flop parade,
Marching along, oh the fun we've made!
Sunscreen fights break out on the shore,
It's only a game, can't wait for more!

Pallet of Dunes and Dreams

Sandy slopes rise like a mountain of fluff,
"We can sled down!" Oh, isn't it tough?
A tumble and roll, giggles fill the air,
Who needs a slide when you've got this fair?

We build castles, but they wash away,
"Let's make a moat!" What a splashing display!
Buckets and shovels become high-tech tools,
Defending our turf from those sneaky pool fools.

Whispering Sands

The sands whisper secrets, but I can't hear,
Too busy tossing my last beach beer.
A crab sidesteps with a wink and a grin,
Are his dance moves better? Let's see who'll win!

Tanning in stripes, I'm a zebra supreme,
While my friends play tag, chasing a dream.
Caught in laughter, we spin round and round,
In this silly sea, joy can always be found.

Solitude Beneath Coconut Palms

There once was a crab named Lou,
Who danced like he just had a brew.
He slipped on a shell,
And fell with a yell,
Leaving seagulls to laugh as he flew.

Beneath palms where the coconuts sway,
A parrot would squawk, 'What a day!'
With a wink and a grin,
He'd say, 'Let me in!'
As the sun chased the clouds far away.

Tides of Tranquility

A turtle named Tim enjoyed sun,
He'd lounge all day, oh what fun!
But tides pulled him back,
In a comical act,
He'd roll with the waves, on the run.

With each little splash, what a sight,
He'd tip over, laughing with might.
As fish giggled near,
It was perfectly clear,
That joy is the true ocean delight.

Driftwood Dreams

On a log that was drifting away,
A raccoon planned his grand buffet.
With snacks piled so high,
He wanted to fly,
But the waves seemed to say, 'Not today!'

He munched on a shell with a smirk,
While pelicans eyed him with work.
'You can't eat that, friend!'
'Tis a trend to upend,'
But he just took a bite with a quirk.

The Ocean's Secret Haven

There's a clam with a pearl who can sing,
Who dreams of one day growing wings.
He croons through the tide,
With fish by his side,
Creating the ocean's own fling.

Along came a shrimp, oh so spry,
'Join me!' he said with a sigh.
Together they'd dance,
In each silly prance,
As jellyfish floated on by.

Sunsets Unbound

On a beach made of gummy bears,
The seagulls squawk in pastel flares.
Sandy toes and sunburned noses,
We'll dance with crabs, oh how it poses!

As jellyfish wave their tentacle flags,
We giggle as the tide steals our rags.
Sun melts down in a splashing spree,
We laugh so hard, we can't find our tea!

With flip-flops on the wrong way round,
We chase odd fish that hop and bound.
Caught in a limbo, we twist and groove,
It's just the sun and us in the move!

The coconut drinks, they come with umbrellas,
While we juggle fruit, quite the fella.
Adventure awaits in our silly plays,
As the sun dips down and brings on rays.

Oasis of Quietude

In a hammock made of licorice lace,
I nap with a crab wearing sunglasses on his face.
The coconuts whisper a sleepy tune,
While the flamingos strut, oh they swoon!

A goat in flip-flops is quite a sight,
He dances and twirls in the fading light.
I sip my drink while the parrot squawks,
'You dance like you've got sauce in your socks!'

With every breeze a new joke takes flight,
As I unsuccessfully take aim at a kite.
The sea laughs at my fishing skills,
I catch a boot, but it doesn't bring thrills!

So let's toast to the waves, the giggles, the fun,
With the sun like a pancake, oh boy, how it's done!
A place where the troubles just slip and slide,
In this laughter-filled nook, let's all abide.

Tranquil Shores Await

On shores where the laughter meets the sand,
The crabs organize a marching band.
With seashells bright and starfish that dance,
We twirl in the water, lost in a trance!

The seagulls steal chips, oh what a heist!
While I ponder if seaweed's a tasty feast item or a vice.
Belly flops and waves, my friends are in stitches,
We embrace the absurd, no time for glitches!

The dolphins giggle and wave us along,
While I sing off-key to a corky song.
The tide pulls us in, then back to the sky,
With my sunhat askew and my favorite tie!

So come join the fun, let your worries float,
We'll build a fortress made of candy, on a whim we wrote.
Each giggle and splash, a sweet cocoon,
In this silly place under the mischievous moon.

Beyond the Currents

Where the sun sneezes gold upon the waves,
And the fish wear hats, it's all that it braves.
A kite flies by, it's stuck to my drink,
But in this ruckus, I'll never blink!

With surfboards painted like rainbows of cheer,
We laugh at the waves and forget all our fear.
The tide swirls in, trying to steal my snacks,
But I shout, 'Not today, you silly flax!'

Sandcastles tumble with a mighty roar,
As we escape the deep - what a score!
Banana peels slip, and we all take a dive,
In this absurd realm, we feel so alive!

So here's to the moments of laughter and zest,
Where we'll eat cake for breakfast and wear socks as a vest.
With shouts filling the air and a laugh that's contagious,
Our hearts skip a beat, how joyously outrageous!

Serenity's Lullaby

The waves sing a tune from the sea,
While crabs crawl around, it's quite the spree.
With a coconut hat and a laugh so loud,
I dance with a fish, oh how proud!

The sun's so bright, it tickles my nose,
A seagull steals fries as everyone knows.
With each dive and splash, my worries take flight,
In this wacky paradise, everything's right.

I snooze in a hammock, a sight to behold,
Dreaming of pirates and treasures of gold.
But wait, what's that? A wave rolls in fast,
And wakes me up just to be quite the blast!

So let's build a castle from sand, not from strife,
Where the moat's just a puddle, but full of life.
With laughter and joy, we'll pass the day,
Where shenanigans rule, come laugh and play!

Beyond the Horizon's Hold

Off sails a boat with a goofy grin,
While fish jump around, it's a silly din.
My buddy the whale does a flip and a flop,
Together we make quite the non-stop bop!

The drinks are too fruity, with umbrellas galore,
I sip, then I fall – a splash to the shore!
My sunglasses flipped, but I'm still full of glee,
As a crab laughs along, saying, 'You'll see!'

The sunset paints pinks, with oranges bright,
I miss the best selfies - what a funny sight!
But the laughter and joy are all that I need,
With friends all around, it's a life guaranteed!

The horizon's now faded, yet I still wear a grin,
Exploring our world where the fun never ends.
We'll chase after night, 'til the next silly dawn,
Where laughter and joy are forever reborn!

Elysium in the Breeze

The breeze brings a joke from a dandelion,
As it tickles my nose, I can't help but whine.
A parrot tells tales of adventures gone wrong,
In this kingdom of fun, you can't help but belong!

A crab on a skateboard rolls past with flair,
While I try to catch it, oh what a scare!
The sand's got its own slip-and-slide plan,
And suddenly, I've fallen, oh man, oh man!

The sun's doing the cha-cha, quite out of sync,
As I sip on a smoothie, a bright shade of pink.
With laughter and giggles, we paint the bright day,
In our breezy retreat, where silly hearts play.

My flip-flops get stuck in the sugary sand,
While a beach ball escapes right from my hand.
Chasing after fun, with a hop and a skip,
Here laughs are the treasures, not gold or a trip!

Forgotten Shores

On shores where the grass is too tangled to see,
I trip over laughter, it's always quite free.
My metal detector, it beeps with delight,
But all I find is shells and a kite stuck tight!

A sandcastle rises, but the tide has its say,
It's like we're in the midst of a big ocean play.
With a twist and a turn, the sand crumbles down,
But in this grand mess, we all wear a crown!

The seagulls are eyeing my sandwich with glee,
They flap and they squawk, making fun at me.
I barter my chips for a laugh and a snack,
In this kooky retreat, no fun we'll lack!

At dusk, the beachcombers gather to chat,
About whales with wigs and a cat in a hat.
With laughter as currency, we're rich, can't you see?
On these forgotten shores, we are all wild and free!

Serenity at the Water's Edge

The sun's a cheeky little friend,
It tickles toes and won't pretend.
A crab in shorts, he struts about,
While seagulls laugh and flail about.

A beach ball bounces, dodges waves,
It's a game of tag, the ball misbehaves.
Sandy footprints, a playful chase,
Lost flip-flops find a special place.

The tide rolls in, a sneaky thief,
A picnic basket, now in grief.
Grapes float by, a fruity spree,
Cheers to the waves, they set us free!

With sand in hair, we dance and sway,
Who needs a plan? Let's shout hooray!
The ocean's giggles fill the air,
As laughter skips without a care.

Dreams Adrift on Gentle Currents

A rubber ducky leads the way,
On a raft made of hay, oh yay!
Sunscreen surfers, slick and spry,
Dive into joy with a cheerful sigh.

Floating on dreams, we wave and splash,
With mermaids plotting a silly crash.
Their laughter echoes, a bubbly tune,
Bubbles popping like a cartoon!

The jellyfish wobble, a jig so grand,
As fish wear hats, they form a band.
A crab conducts with a tiny claw,
Their symphony plucks a funny flaw.

With snacks that crumble, sand is fine,
We build a fortress, toast with brine.
Life's a feast, so grab a bite,
On this wacky ride, all feels right!

Horizon's Gentle Caress

The horizon winks, a flirty tease,
While flip-flops squeak with the salty breeze.
A lone coconut tries to roll,
It's off to its own comical stroll.

Tangled in seaweed, a beach dog barks,
As I laugh at his aquatic sparks.
A wave crashes, friends take flight,
Splashing water, oh what a sight!

Surfers chase shadows, silly indeed,
Balancing dreams on boards at speed.
A seagull swoops with a daring dive,
Stealing fries, oh what a jive!

Tides whisper secrets in evening hues,
Under the stars, we light our shoes.
With dance and laughter, we greet the night,
Holding onto joy, embracing delight.

A Tale of Salty Air

Salty air tickles my nose,
While I dance like a seaweed rose.
A dolphin giggles, flips with grace,
Waves crash down, a foamy race.

The lifeguard's chair, a throne so high,
Where seagulls conspire and swoop by.
With towels tangled, we strike a pose,
In the warmth where fun never close.

An icy treat, I take a lick,
A seagull steals it, what a trick!
Sandcastles rise, but then they fall,
A waterfall of giggles, we all haul.

The sun sets low, like a curtain call,
We gather 'round, our laughter a wall.
In this tale, under stars so bright,
We savor this fun, with all our might.

Serenity Among the Tides

The sun was bright, the drinks were cold,
With laughter shared, we felt quite bold.
A seagull swooped, my lunch in tow,
And now I'm stuck with just a glow.

The waves crashed down, they tickled my feet,
A fish swam by, it looked so neat.
I tried to dance, my flip-flops flew,
Instead of grace, I made a stew.

A crab waltzed in, my dancing partner,
We spun like tops, oh what a charmer!
But then he pinched, and I gave a shout,
Serenity? More like a bout!

The sun sets low, we wave goodbye,
With sandy feet, we touch the sky.
From tides of joy to crabs' surprise,
I'll always laugh at my beach ties.

Voyage to Nowhere

I hopped on a boat, no map in sight,
A crew of ducks seemed just right.
We set sail with snacks in hand,
Heading off to...oh, wasn't planned.

With jellyfish waving, the fish looked bored,
"Is this the place?" we all adored.
I thought of treasure, I sought some gold,
But found a sock that smelled quite bold.

The ducks quacked loud, "We've lost our way!"
All we saw were waves of gray.
No destination in our scheme,
A voyage reminiscent of a dream.

As stars appeared, we made a tune,
Dancing along under the moon.
Next time I'll pack a proper chart,
For now, I'll just enjoy the art!

Coconuts and Clouds

I climbed a tree for a coconut prize,
Tripped on a root, met the ground, what a surprise!
Coconuts rolled, the birds just laughed,
I pondered life, it must be craft.

My hat flew off in a gentle breeze,
An octopus waved, "Hey, want some cheese?"
I dreamt of clouds, fluffy and bright,
But fell face-first, what a sight!

With every stumble, I sparked a smile,
Tickled by sand, I stayed for a while.
The clouds above were cotton candy sweet,
As I dined on fish, it was quite a treat.

If coconuts dropped like confetti rain,
I'd dance with joy, feel no shame.
For laughter lives where troubles flee,
In my coconuts and clouds, fancy-free!

The Comfort of Isolation

I built a hut with sticks and sand,
Just for me, it's perfectly planned.
The parrot squawked, "You're all alone!"
I shrugged and said, "Just me and my bone!"

No one to fight over beach chairs here,
Just me and my snacks, nothing to fear.
The tide rolls in, I tie my shoe,
A wave said, "Boo!" and I just flew!

The sun beats down, a tan I'll gain,
Until the crabs come to stake their claim.
They scuttle up, expect a feast,
But all I serve is my thoughts released.

Isolation's fun, it's true, I say,
With no one here to ruin my day.
So bring on the laughs, the solitude wide,
For in my own world, I truly abide.

Where the Sea Meets the Sky

On a boat that won't float, what a sight,
Caught a fish that was quite a fright.
It jumped and it splashed, oh what a splash,
I slipped on the deck and it was quite the crash.

With my sunscreen applied, I look like a ghost,
Seagulls above, they laugh at me most.
I dance with the waves, my shoes in the tide,
While the crabs on the sand choose to run and hide.

The sun is a beacon; my hat flies away,
Chasing it down, oh what a ballet!
Flip-flops a-flying, I run like a fool,
In this silly game, I'm the unwitting jewel.

But laughter erupts as I trip on a shell,
The ocean waves cheer, they know me so well.
With salty seas air and mischief in tow,
Life's funny like this, just go with the flow.

Tranquil Retreats

A hammock that sways in the fresh ocean breeze,
I'm not napping; I'm trying to seize!
The moment, I swear, then I snore oh so loud,
While the waves roll in, the seagulls are proud.

My drink with a topping of little fruit hats,
A cocktail that's more like a science of spats.
With little umbrellas that flare in the sun,
I sip through a straw—it's a laugh and a pun!

On this sandy retreat, a game of charades,
I'm a fish and a crab, oh the great masquerades!
My friends join the fray, twirling around,
We flop like a fish, hitting the ground!

As dusk rolls in, the laughter won't cease,
Under twinkling stars, we toast to our peace.
With giggles and grins, this day we'll embrace,
In our tranquil retreat, we've found our true place.

Nature's Hidden Sanctuary

In a jungle that giggles, the vines start to swing,
I follow a bird that's invented a fling.
It chirps like a comedian, hopping with flair,
While I trip on a root—does nature beware?

A waterfall whispers, it tickles my toes,
The frogs in the reeds wear comical clothes.
They croak out their jokes, ribbit over and over,
As I slip on a rock—I'm a slippery rover!

The trees are like giants, they watch me with glee,
While monkeys swing by, throwing coconuts at me!
"Just sharing our snacks!" they shout with a grin,
And I laugh as I dodge, trying not to spin.

In this hidden retreat, where the wild critters play,
I'm the punchline of jokes, but hey, that's okay!
For in nature's embrace, I find laughter and cheer,
In this sanctuary wild, I shed every fear.

Solace Amongst the Sea

With floaties like dolphins, I splash and I laugh,
A pool noodle party, the silliest staff.
The sun is my DJ, the waves is the bass,
We groove with the seagulls; they dance with grace.

In a kayak that wobbles, I paddle about,
Look ma, I'm a captain—without any doubt!
But a wave gives a push and I'm splashing around,
With fishies now giggling from under the sound.

A treasure hunt's on with maps drawn in sand,
But I found only jelly, not gold at hand.
The crabs cheer me on as I dig like a fool,
They scuttle in laughter; "These tides must be cruel!"

But as sunsets arrive, painting skies all aglow,
I chuckle and grin, for it's all quite the show.
Amongst the cool sea, where troubles drift free,
I find my solace, just laughing with glee.

Rest in the Palms

Swaying high above, the coconuts sing,
Lizards on surfboards, ready for spring.
Crabs doing the cha-cha, shells in a line,
Even the sand says, "Hey, this is fine!"

Sunburnt tourists in search of a tan,
Forget the sunscreen, that was the plan!
With piña coladas, we're feeling no pain,
At least till tomorrow, when it starts to rain.

The Driftwood Diary

A stick wrote a story, driftwood and sea,
It said, "Life's a beach, come laugh with me!"
A fish in a tutu danced on the shore,
Said, "Join me, my friend, for a good, silly score!"

Seagulls are cackling, a comical flock,
Stealing our fries, oh, isn't that the shock?
We giggle and chuckle as waves take the bait,
Just hope that they don't show up on our plate!

Breath of the Open Sea

The sea's a giant who breathes in and out,
With bubbles of laughter, no need for a doubt.
Mermaids with giggles, they twist and they twirl,
"Come on in, silly, let's give it a whirl!"

Surfers are tumbling like logs in a rush,
Waves scoff and chuckle, creating a hush.
Seashells are whispering tales spun of glee,
In a world where we all can just flop like the sea.

Nurtured by Nature

Under the sun, with a coconut drink,
Mother Nature's laughing, don't you agree?
Bamboo grows taller, a ticklish embrace,
As koalas do karaoke, what a wild place!

In the shade of the palm, a scorpion winks,
Dancing with iguanas, no time for Sphinx.
Cucumber in hand, we're chilling with flair,
Nature's great party, so much zest in the air!

Port of Lost Souls

Sailing into a harbor of mismatched socks,
Drunken parrots squawking, stealing your rocks.
The captain's hat is askew on his head,
While fish in top hats dance, a ball to be fed.

A chef cooks with seaweed, a curious fare,
Claiming it's gourmet, though it smells like despair.
Seagulls hold meetings, plotting to dive,
While crabs in a conga line aim to survive.

Throw a rope, catch a buoy, swim with delight,
But watch for the jellyfish, they bite just for spite.
With treasure maps drawn in crayon and glue,
Every wrong turn leads to a party for two.

At dusk, the mermaids sing, off-key but sweet,
Soliciting sailors with their dance and their feet.
A ruckus ensues as the moon takes its role,
In this port of chaos, a ball that's a troll.

Swells of Freedom

Waves that giggle and bubble with glee,
Surfboards made of pizza, oh how lucky are we!
The dolphins dance, wearing sunglasses with flair,
While turtles in flip-flops rock out without care.

Sandy castles outshine the finest of bling,
Where throw pillows fight for the title of king.
A drought of proper etiquette, see how they spin,
As crabs serving cocktails invite you to join in.

Seashells with gossip and secrets to share,
Chasing the gulls and the fish in mid-air.
Life jackets made of marshmallows, what a delight,
Splashing in swells that glow neon at night.

The ocean's our playground, no rules only fun,
Under a shower of milkshakes and sun.
Here's to the surf, the sand, and the cheer,
In swells of freedom, we'll dance without fear!

Beneath the Shade of the Banyan

Beneath the branches that tickle our toes,
We nap with the breeze, as everybody knows.
The monkeys perform in a slapstick parade,
While lizards in sunglasses engage in charades.

Picnics with sandwiches shaped like a fish,
Each bite is a gamble; oh, how we all wish.
Ants debut their dance routine to impress,
While bees buzz in chorus, adding to the mess.

The banyan is gossiping, spreading the word,
Of tourists who trip on three-legged bird.
In this shade of hilarity, nonsense erupts,
With coconuts rolling, as laughter erupts.

As sunset approaches, the fun must remain,
Dancing with shadows, ignoring all pain.
We toast with our cola, life's simple and grand,
Beneath the shade, let's all take a stand!

The Calm Before the Storm

A quiet like whispers, a breeze with a snicker,
Palm trees are giggling, the sun's growing thicker.
Fish in a frenzy, they've all found their groove,
While seashells are plotting a cha-cha move.

Waves with a smirk, they roll in with cheer,
Just waiting for raindrops to pop up, oh dear!
The sky looks suspicious, as gray as a mime,
While lightning winks cheekily, counting its time.

The coconuts chuckle, they know what awaits,
A splash of adventure with unpredictable fates.
Umbrellas are hiding in fear from the sight,
As stripes of wild wind prepare for a fight.

So raise up your hands and your hopes to the sky,
Dance in the puddles, don't question the why.
Embrace the surprise in this wild weather twist,
For the calm may be funny, much more than you wished!

Tidal Dreams

The waves dance silly, like spry young pups,
Chasing the sun in their watery jumps.
Seagulls squawk tales of snack attacks,
While crabby critters plan their next snacks.

A coconut smiles as it rolls on by,
Saying hello with a wavering sigh.
Sand castles lean, then tumble and crash,
As the tide giggles, oh what a splash!

Shells whisper secrets of tides gone past,
While mermaids chuckle, their laughter is vast.
The sun winks down at the playful scene,
As beachgoers wonder where all the ice cream's been.

Dancing on towels like quirky ballet,
With jellyfish floats, we sway and sway.
The sunscreen's sticky, but oh what a thrill,
In this sunny madness, we find our fill.

Encounters with Serenity

Serenity struts with a goofy grin,
Waves crashing like laughter from deep within.
Sandy toes wiggle in rhythm with glee,
While turtles in shades sip their iced tea.

The horizon wears a bewildered shade,
A fish in a bow tie joins the parade.
From flippers to fins, they join the fun,
In a wacky dance under the sun.

Drifting on breezes that tickle our nose,
We chase after rainbows, we giggle and pose.
The surfboard's a skateboard, and we ride like pros,
While waves try to splash us in colorful clothes.

In twilight's glow, we gather around,
Sharing tall tales that make silly sound.
With laughter like bubbles, we soar and we sing,
In this goofy dream where bliss is the king.

Midday Escape

Sun hats are tilted, drinks in our hands,
We're ready for mischief, in sun-soaked lands.
The beach ball rolls like a runaway kite,
While sunscreen struggles to keep skin bright.

We build up the laughter, then let down our hair,
As the seagulls plot snacks that we don't want to share.
Tanned bunnies hop with a bounce and a spring,
While sandy feet find joy in the silly things.

With a splash and a giggle, life's worries are few,
As we dance in a circle, all covered in goo.
The sun starts to yawn, the shadows get long,
Yet our hearts only sing a most joyful song.

Midday delights in this wacky charade,
As the tide tickles toes beneath palm tree shade.
In this frolicsome chaos, we find our way,
With laughter and waves, we'll seize the day!

Adrift on Azure

Floating in bliss on this bumpy old raft,
Where laughter's the currency and joy's the craft.
A fish wears a hat and waves as it swims,
While we crack up, blessed by the ocean's whims.

Sky and sea blend in a hilarious fight,
Clouds wear pink pajamas, what a sight!
With beach umbrellas dancing to a beat,
And crabs in tuxedos offer snacks, what a treat!

Time ticks slowly in this comical space,
As dolphins unite in a friendly race.
With sunscreen on noses and sand in our hair,
We trade silly stories without any care.

The horizon giggles, the sunsets applaud,
As we wade through our laughter, delightfully flawed.
Adrift on this azure, we dance like the tide,
With hearts full of joy, we happily glide.

Where the Sun Dances

The sun wears shades, oh what a sight,
A flamingo dance, in pure delight.
Cocktails clink as seagulls squawk,
Join the conga, let's all rock!

Flip-flops flying, a dog with a hat,
A crab shuffle, what's up with that?
Surfers tumble like a jolly clown,
Even the fish are laughing now!

The palm trees sway, doing the twist,
A piña colada you can't resist.
With jellyfish that moonwalk, it's clear,
We're all here just for some cheer!

So pack up your troubles, leave them behind,
Join the parade, let's unwind!
When life's a joke, don't take it too hard,
Life's just a beach, let down your guard!

Refuge in the Salt Breeze

A rubber ducky floats in the bay,
Squeaks out jokes in a sunny array.
The sandcastle king wears a crown made of shells,
While laughter echoes, our fun repels.

The crabs are doing the cha-cha, oh dear,
A beach ball bounces, spreading good cheer.
With ice cream dripping on sunburnt toes,
Who needs a plan? Let the fun just flow!

A snail hugs a surfboard, dreams of a ride,
While dolphins say hello with a flip and glide.
The salty breeze whispers funny retorts,
Even the sharks are wearing beach shorts!

With flip-flops flapping, we run to the shore,
Chasing our worries, we laugh even more!
When the sun's shining bright, there's nothing to lose,
Just gather your pals and cut loose!

Sheltered by the Sea

In a hammock strung with laughter and sighs,
A parrot mimics, oh what a surprise!
The sun's our waiter, brings drinks on a tray,
Even the sand crabs are ready to play!

A coconut lands, and we all duck down,
The beach ball's a comet that's lost in the town.
Waves break in giggles; they tickle our toes,
With salt in our hair, we strike silly poses!

The clam's a maestro, conducts with a shell,
While a jellyfish rolls in a trance-like spell.
Seashells exchange the juiciest goss,
"Did you hear? Sally's got a new gloss!"

We're sheltered here; the ocean's our friend,
With waves hitched to laughter that never will end.
So join in the flotsam, let's swim with the light,
In this funny old paradise, everything's right!

Nautical Reverie

A pirate ship that lost its map,
Found treasure chests filled with candy and crap.
A mermaid's giggle, a fish in a tie,
Swapping tall tales as gulls zoom by.

With octopuses juggling colorful balls,
A hippo in sunglasses having beach brawls.
The seaweed dances, it's quite a sight,
While crabby chefs show off their seafood fight!

The sun's the captain, steering the cheer,
Life's a bit wavy, we steer from our fears.
In this dream afloat, with sand on our feet,
All aboard for laughter, what a treat!

With a parrot on my shoulder, all smiles in sight,
We toast to the sky and let spirits take flight.
So let's sail on this wave of fun unaware,
In this nautical dream, all troubles will wear!

Echoes of the Forgotten Cove

In a cove where coconuts sway,
Beach towels fly in the sun's ray,
Seagulls squawk with witty flair,
As tourists try to balance their hair.

The crabs dance with mischief galore,
Sneaking snacks off the sandy shore,
While sunburned folks count their toes,
Chasing shadows as the ocean flows.

A flip-flop thrown, a screeching parrot,
Their vacation plans go awry like a carrot,
Yet laughter rings through salty air,
As fish blush at the beachgoers' dare.

With sunscreen smears, they've lost the fight,
But still wave goodbye to the sunset light,
In this cove where the absurd takes stage,
They'll return again, full of laughter and rage.

Whispers of the Ocean's Heart

Shells and laughter echo so bright,
As beach chairs wobble in a hilarious sight,
A crab in shades struts down the line,
Giving beach bums a hard time to dine.

The waves giggle, rolling in neat,
Tickling toes as tourists retreat,
While sunscreen battles against a sneeze,
Creating chaos on the warm sea breeze.

With each splash, a new joke's told,
As jellyfish taunt with a sting so bold,
Flippers on, the rescue awaits,
While swimmers argue, it's all in good fates.

So here they gather, stories to share,
In the whispers of sea foam, all without care,
As evening falls with a laugh and a cheer,
They'll return for more chaos, year after year.

A Solitary Sailor's Escape

A sailor set sail with a wink and a grin,
In a boat that was more of a tin can spin,
With a map upside down, oh what a sight,
He steered for the horizon, but not quite right.

The fish had a jolly old time at his plight,
Jumping and flopping, quite the delight,
While he pondered if mermaids served tea,
In waters where he lost his sense of glee.

His compass was broken, he'd swear it was fun,
Chasing shadows as the day turned to sun,
With seagulls mocking his nautical skills,
He laughed as he drifted on whimsical thrills.

So he sailed along, fueled by a dream,
Wondering if this was all what it seemed,
In the solitude of waves and the quirk of the sea,
He found laughter in mischief; now he sails with glee.

Twilight Over Turquoise Waters

As the sun dips low, the waters gleam,
A party of dolphins plots a wild scheme,
To boogie with fish under the moon's glance,
While beachgoers stumble in a clumsy dance.

With ice-cream cones that are drippy and neat,
The kids run around with quick little feet,
As sandcastles tumble in a giggling spree,
Their sandy pirate ships sailing on glee.

A hammock sways as the evening unfolds,
Where stories of blunders and laughter are told,
As the twilight whispers, inviting the stars,
While mosquitoes plot in a dance full of bars.

Yet here they sit, with smiles so wide,
In a charming chaos, a joy-filled ride,
With twilight as backdrop to their wild tales,
They'll treasure these moments as ocean prevails.

Memories of a Distant Cove

I found a crab that danced with glee,
He waved his claws while mocking me.
A seagull stole my sandwich, bold,
I laughed it off, my lunch is sold.

The sunscreen squirted, made me slip,
I landed right in Grandma's grip.
She grinned and said, 'Now that's a spot!'
I blushed as I became a dot!

The jellyfish parade, what a sight,
They jiggled and wiggled with sheer delight.
In flip-flops lost, I ran like mad,
Chasing my shoes, oh, it was rad!

With sand in my shorts and salt in my hair,
I strutted around without any care.
Memories made in sun and fun,
I'll cherish them all, each and every one.

Beneath the Coconut Sky

The coconuts dropped without a sound,
I ducked and dashed on the sandy ground.
A monkey swung and stole my hat,
I chased him off, yelling like a brat.

My friends were building castles tall,
But a wave crashed down—oh, not at all!
'You call that a moat?' I couldn't help tease,
As they shrieked and squealed, then fell to their knees.

The stars at night made me feel so grand,
Except for the ones that brought quicksand.
'Oh look!', I said, 'An outdoor bed!'
Then found out, nope, it's where dreams go dead!

Under that sky, we danced like fools,
Splashing about in a race of drools.
A coconut punch my buddy did throw,
But in the end, it's laughter that will grow.

Retreat from the World

The world's chaos faded far away,
As we lounged in hammocks, all work at bay.
I spilled my drink and got a tan,
A lizard laughed, called me 'The Beach Man!'

We played hide and seek with fish and shrimps,
While yelling at the seagulls for being blimps.
A crab joined us, made quite the fuss,
Demanding snacks and catching every bus.

Oh, what joy to forget the grind,
With a flip-flop lost, and a drink unkind.
The sun set low, with a purple hue,
I realized, this chaos is just for a view!

We toasted our drinks and danced in the sand,
Swapping more stories than we ever planned.
Tomorrow's trouble can wait for now,
Let's keep the laughter—oh, take a bow!

The Beauty of Being Lost

With a map in my hand, I started to roam,
But tripped on a shell, it felt like home.
The wind whispered secrets of where I should go,
But I followed a crab that was stealing my toe!

There were seagulls above, with their squawking song,
I think they were plotting; it felt all wrong.
I nodded at tourists, unsure of my place,
As they laughed at my hair, a true jungle grace.

A beach ball bounced and hit me in the cheek,
I joined in the fun, and soon found my peak.
With nothing but giggles and ice cream galore,
I made friends with waves, who couldn't ignore.

Being lost isn't scary, I found it quite neat,
With treasures discovered at each sunny treat.
So here's to the flops, the slips, and the toss,
In this wondrous chaos, I found my gloss!

Barefoot Wanderlust

I left my shoes upon the shore,
With toes in sand, I crave for more.
The crabs and I, we dance and prance,
In a spontaneous summer chance.

A seagull stole my last fry snack,
Now I plot my pigeon attack.
With laughter loud, I chase the breeze,
And let the waves tickle my knees.

The sun's hot glow is quite a sight,
I tried to tan; thus, lost my fight.
My burnt red nose is proof, you see,
No one should trust my SPF three.

But who needs shoes when life is bright,
With belly laughs and pure delight?
In flip-flops or just bare and free,
This carefree heart beats joyfully.

A Refuge in Cerulean

In waters blue, like skies above,
I seek a place where laughter's love.
Inflatable flamingos float around,
As I dodge a pesky seagull's sound.

The coconut drinks, they bring me cheer,
I sip too fast; oh dear, oh dear!
A paper umbrella in my cup,
Just adds to the fun as I fill up.

I spot a crab with swagger bold,
As it struts by, I can't help but scold.
'You think you're cool, but I'm the show!'
And then it pinches; oh no, oh no!

With friends who giggle, dance like fish,
We conjure dreams, fulfilled by wish.
In the cerulean sun's warm glow,
We find our refuge and let joy flow.

Secrets of the Coral Cove

In a cove where secrets softly sway,
Fish gossip while turtles play.
I stumbled on a seashell parade,
Thought it was serious; I was dismayed.

A starfish winked, as if in jest,
I laughed so hard, I lost my vest!
With all its arms, it took a hold,
Forcing me to join the fold.

Dolphins danced through waves with glee,
I tried to join; they laughed at me.
In a whirl of bubbles, oh what fun,
I pretended I was also a ton!

But as the sun began to sink,
I found my friends, we shared a drink.
The coral secrets whispered so sweet,
In this silly cove, joy felt complete.

Palm Shadows at Dusk

As evening paints the sky with gold,
I find palm shadows, bold and cold.
They stretch and yawn while I sip soda,
A coconut smile straight from the moda!

On the sand, I write my name,
The tide comes in; oh, what a game!
It swallows letters with a sigh,
At least my hand prints are now dry.

Nearby, a parrot squawks with flair,
I mimic back; it gives me a stare.
'You're not a bird!' it on loops repeat,
But I just laugh at the cheeky feat.

As night descends, the stars awake,
With my pals, we munch on cake.
With palm tree shadows playing tricks,
We dance and giggle, night-time flicks.

www.ingramcontent.com/pod-product-compliance
Lightning Source LLC
Chambersburg PA
CBHW072134070526
44585CB00016B/1680